Letters and Sounds

-un, -ut, -up

Harcourt

SCHOOL PUBLISHERS

Photos:
p. 2, © Harcourt Telescope; p. 3, © Harcourt Index; p. 4, © Harcourt Index; p. 5, © Harcourt Telescope; p. 6, © Superstock; p. 7, © Harcourt Telescope; p. 8, © Superstock.

Printed in China

ISBN-13: 978-0-15-358384-1
ISBN-10: 0-15-358384-3

Ordering Options
ISBN 10: 0-15-358355-X (Grade K Below-Level Collection)
ISBN 13: 978-0-15-358355-1 (Grade K Below-Level Collection)
ISBN 10: 0-15-360637-1 (package of 5)
ISBN 13: 978-0-15-360637-3 (package of 5)

4 5 6 7 8 9 10 0940 15 14 13 12 11 10 09

sun

nut

run

up

bun

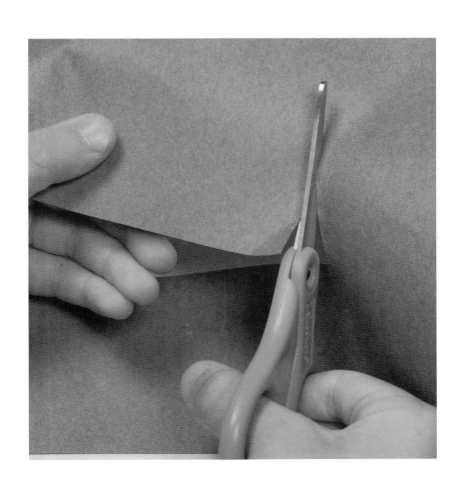

cut

cup